Geronimo

by

Tanya Landman

Illustrated by Seb Camagajevac

With thanks to Leland Michael Darrow, tribal historian, Fort Sill Apache tribe, Oklahoma.

First published in 2010 in Great Britain by
Barrington Stoke Ltd
18 Walker St, Edinburgh, EH3 7LP

www.barringtonstoke.co.uk

Photo of Geronimo in 1887 on p. 68, by Ben Wittick, Archival Research Catalog of the National Archives and Records Administration

Photo of Geronimo and warriors in 1886 on p. 69 courtesy of Arizona Historical Society

ISBN: 978-1-84299-753-6

Printed in Great Britain by Bell & Bain Ltd

Contents

Introduction

Picture this.

You come home one day and there are new people living in your house. You don't know them. But they've moved in. Taken over.

While you've been at school they've chopped down the tree in the garden and dug up the grass. They've made a bonfire with your stuff. They say your home belongs to them. They've got a piece of paper to prove it. They want you out. NOW. And they've got guns. If you don't leave, they'll kill you.

"But where can I go?" you ask them.

That's when they show you a map. They point to the place you've got to live in from now on. It's down on the waste land near the stinking canal. One of them lifts his gun to your head. His eyes are cold. Cruel. His finger's on the trigger. He's going to pull it. You've got no choice. You go.

When you get to the waste land you find there are soldiers all around it. These people have got their own army! Once you're through the gates you can't leave.

Everyone you know seems to be crammed on to that little plot of ground – even the gang from the year above you at school. You've hated them since Year 7. One of them has already got in a fight with a mate of yours. They're throwing punches at each other. Your mate's nose has started to bleed.

Your belly rumbles. You haven't had tea. You look around. There's nothing to eat and even if there was food there's no way to cook it.

You're thirsty. But there's nothing to drink. Some people have started taking water from the canal but you know it's dirty. Toxic. If you swallow that, it'll kill you. That's if you don't die of cold first. There's no shelter anywhere – not so much as a shed to sleep in.

What do you do? Do you give in? Starve? Die?

Or do you fight?

How far would you go to defend your freedom?

Chapter 1
Geronimo!

"Geronimo!"

You'll have heard that name before. It's what the movie hero shouts when he jumps off the roof of a burning building.

It's what people in books scream when they leap across a huge gap.

People yell "*Geronimo!*" when they're doing something scary. The idea started in World War Two. Some American soldiers were watching a cowboy film the night before a dangerous mission. The soldiers were paratroopers. In the film there was an Indian warrior called Geronimo. He had to jump off a high cliff right down into a river. As he leapt, he yelled his name.

After the film, one of the paratroopers said he'd shout out "Geronimo!" as he jumped out of the plane the next day. That would prove he wasn't scared! The trend caught on. It's now the official motto of that group of soldiers – the 501st Parachute Infantry Regiment.

But Geronimo wasn't the real name of that Indian. When he was born in 1829 in what's now known as New Mexico, his parents called him Goyathlay – "one who yawns".

Geronimo was a Chiricahua Apache Indian. The bravery and skill of all Apache fighters was well-known. But Geronimo became the most famous of them all.

At that time there were many different Apache tribes. Each tribe was split into small groups, or bands, of families and each one had its own chief. Some tribes were farmers but most hunted deer and other animals.

They also picked the fruits, roots, nuts and seeds that grew wild.

The Apache god was called Ussen. He was the creator and life giver. Ussen gave each tribe a home-land and everything that they needed was there.

It was a gentle, peaceful life, but there were dangers – mountain lions and bears, rattle-snakes, poisonous spiders and scorpions. There were months with no rain at all and then flash floods. Dust storms, wild-fires and blizzards sometimes swept across their land. And the Apaches had many enemies.

Children learnt survival skills when they were very young. As a small boy Geronimo knew where to find water in the dry desert. He knew how to ride and hunt and how to make a fire. He knew how to move across the land with astonishing speed.

Children practised their skills. Sometimes they took a mouthful of water and ran for miles without spilling or swallowing it. They played "creep and freeze" – sneaking up on each other without being seen.

Geronimo knew how to crouch down and stay perfectly still so that from far away he looked like a rock. He knew how to leap from stone to stone so that he left no trail. Like all Apaches, he could melt into the landscape so well that his enemies thought he'd become invisible.

Geronimo learnt how to hide. But he also learnt how to fight.

He knew how to fire arrows from his bow and how to use a lance. Apache boys tested their strength in wrestling matches against each other. They had mock battles armed with slings and rocks.

Sometimes the men left the camp on an expedition. They might need to find food for their families. They might be going to fight an enemy. The older boys often went with them. They had to look after the horses and cook the meals.

Four was an important number to the Apaches.

When a boy had made his fourth journey, and if he had done well, the men would agree he was now an adult.

Geronimo was just seventeen when he came back from his fourth journey and joined the tribe's council. Soon after, he married the woman he loved. Her name was Alope, and they had children.

Geronimo said, "We were happy."

It didn't last.

In 1850 the Apaches' old enemy shattered Geronimo's happiness. In one terrible attack the Mexicans gave him a hunger for revenge that lasted for the rest of his life.

Chapter 2
The Mexicans

The Apaches and the Mexicans had been enemies for a very long time. It had started over 300 years before when the Spanish invaded Mexico and said the land was theirs. The Spanish then moved north, towards what is now called Arizona and New Mexico. They killed the Indians who lived there or made them slaves.

Arizona and New Mexico was Apache territory. The Apaches stayed free by moving into the mountains. But there weren't as many animals to hunt as there had been on the grassy plains. To keep their families from starving they sometimes raided Mexican villages and took cattle and horses.

The Spanish tried to get rid of all the Apaches. They failed. 300 years later, the Mexicans tried to finish off what the Spanish had started and kill all the Indians. People thought that taking scalps was an Apache custom. It wasn't. It was the Mexicans' idea to cut the skin and hair off the heads of their dead enemies. Their government paid high prices for Apache scalps.

But in the summer of 1850 the Apaches were at peace with the Mexicans. Geronimo, Alope and their three small children travelled south with the rest of the tribe to trade with them.

One day when the men were away from the camp Mexican troops rode in. They killed everyone they found there. Geronimo's mother, his wife and three children died in the attack.

The tribe were deep inside Mexican-held territory. The only hope for the Indians still alive was to escape. The Apache chief was Mangas Coloradas. He told his people to begin their journey at once, leaving the dead where they had fallen. They set off. Geronimo said, "A few days later we arrived at our own settlement ... There were the play-things of our little ones. I burned them all, even our tepee ..." Geronimo said he was never again happy in his home. He had vowed revenge.

Not long after this terrible homecoming Geronimo was given an extraordinary Power.

Power was a gift from the Apache god, Ussen. When Ussen chose someone to work through he gave them special skills.

With different people, Power took different forms. One person might be given Power to heal, another might see into the future, a third might know where the enemy was or where new food supplies could be found. In other Indian tribes Power belonged to just one Medicine Man. In Apache tribes, many people had Power of one kind or another. This made some of their enemies say they were all witches.

Geronimo was sitting alone and weeping for his lost family, when he heard a voice call his name four times. The voice told him that from now on all his arrows would hit their targets. Nothing would hurt him. It promised, "No gun can ever kill you."

A year later, this promise to Geronimo was tested in a battle.

Chapter 3
Revenge

A year after Geronimo's family had been killed three tribes came together for revenge. They were led by three chiefs – Mangas Coloradas, Cochise and Juh.

The Apaches knew that Ussen did not sort out the conflicts between men. It was their job to punish the Mexicans.

Geronimo was the only man who'd lost all his family. He was chosen to direct the attack.

Apaches were famous for killing without being seen. They ambushed their enemies. But this fight with the Mexicans was an open battle.

The Mexicans had guns. The Apaches had bows and arrows, lances and knives. Many of them died. But Geronimo attacked with such force that the Mexican soldiers were terrified of him. The promise Ussen had made was kept. No bullet hurt him. The Mexican soldiers were terrified. They started to call out in Spanish to Saint Gerome to help them. "Geronimo! Geronimo!"

The Apache fighters began to shout "Geronimo!" too, mocking the Mexicans' fear.

That was when Geronimo got his new name. From that moment he was called Geronimo by Indians and whites alike.

The Mexicans were defeated. The Apache tribes went back to their homes. They knew that justice had been done. But Geronimo wanted more Mexican blood. "I still desired more revenge," he said.

All his life Geronimo hated the Mexicans. But soon after that victory he had another enemy to face. One who would change the Apache way of life forever.

The Americans were coming.

Chapter 4
The Americans

To understand fully what happened to Geronimo and his people you have to travel back in time for over 500 years.

Back then the United States of America didn't exist. People in Europe didn't even know America was there.

500 years ago there was big money to be made if you bought spices from India and sold them in Europe. The problem was that

India was a long way away. It was a dangerous journey by land or sea and it took months.

But then a man called Christopher Columbus had a bold new idea that changed everything. Up until then, nearly everyone thought the world was flat. You would fall off the edge if you went too far. India was about as far east as you dared to sail. No one sailed west. They thought it was just sea all the way to the edge. Beyond that there was nothing but black, empty space.

But Christopher Columbus reckoned the world might be round. He hoped that if he sailed far enough west, he might reach India from the other side.

On August 3, 1492 he set sail. Two months later, he saw land. He thought he'd arrived in India and that the people who came to meet him were Indians. By the time he'd worked out that this wasn't India, and that he'd landed in a new country, the name "Indians" had stuck.

When Christopher Columbus "found" North America, it was a disaster for the more than 500 Indian (or Native American) tribes already living there.

People in Europe heard of the enormous lands across the sea. Some of them thought that if they got there quickly they could make their fortunes. For the next 400 years, wave after wave of settlers came from Europe. Bit by bit, every single one of those 500 tribes had their land taken from them.

By 1850, the settlers reached New Mexico and Arizona.

Apache territory.

But the Apaches weren't going to give up easily. Their fight to keep their land and freedom became one of the most famous "Indian Wars".

Chapter 5
The White Eyes

When the Apaches first saw American settlers they thought the new-comers were disgusting and ugly. Hair grew on their faces and bodies just like animals. But the weirdest thing of all for the dark-eyed Apaches was seeing how pale the settlers' eyes were. They called the new arrivals "White Eyes".

When settlers began to move onto Apache land, at first the Indians were friendly.

Cochise – an important chief – let stage coaches run through his territory. He even gave the new-comers fire-wood.

But in 1861 a young US army officer called George Bascom turned Cochise from the White Eyes' helpful friend into their bitter enemy.

It began when some Apaches attacked a settler's farm and kidnapped a boy. George Bascom thought Cochise and his men had done it. He ordered a meeting. When Cochise arrived, Bascom arrested him. But Cochise hadn't had anything to do with the raid. He drew his knife and slashed his way out of the tent where he was being held. Cochise ran. He dodged the bullets and got away but the men with him weren't so lucky. The US soldiers hanged Cochise's brother and two of his nephews. They were all innocent men.

Cochise was overcome with anger. So was Mangas Coloradas, Geronimo's chief.

Mangas was already an enemy of the White Eyes. He'd once gone on a friendly visit to a miners' camp at Pinos Altos. For no reason at all the miners had tied him to a tree and lashed him with bull whips. To do such a thing to any Apache was shocking. To do such a thing to a chief was criminal. The cruel and stupid White Eyes got what they deserved. Mangas Coloradas and Cochise began to attack settlements and supply trains. Geronimo fought with them. They forced the miners in Pinos Altos to leave the place. Settlers fled away from the territory. The stage post in Apache Pass was deserted. Forts were burnt to the ground by the soldiers as they left.

The chiefs thought they'd won. They thought they'd driven the White Eyes from their land and they could live in peace again. For a short time they were triumphant.

What they didn't know was that the White Eyes had gone to fight another war. They hadn't been beaten by the Apaches. They were fighting their fellow Americans in a bloody civil war.

They soon came back. And this time they came back for good.

In the summer of 1862, 1800 soldiers began to advance into Apache territory. Cochise and Mangas Coloradas waited with their men in the rocks above Apache Pass. Geronimo was with them as they watched the enemy come.

The first few soldiers were ones who'd been sent ahead to scout out the land. The chiefs let them through. Then, on July 14th, an advance party of 122 men entered the pass. The Apaches had guns they'd taken

from the White Eyes. They stayed hidden and shot at the soldiers, killing many of them. They were winning. But then the American army fired cannons at the rocks. No man – no matter how skilful or brave – could fight that kind of weapon. The Apaches had to withdraw.

One of the wounded was Mangas Coloradas. His men carried him to a doctor in Mexico. It was a journey of over 100 miles. They told the doctor that if Mangas didn't get better, everyone in the town would die. The people living there were lucky – Mangas survived.

But the Apaches now knew that they couldn't defeat their new enemy. Mangas's men had been beaten at Apache Pass. He couldn't stop the soldiers marching through their home-land. The only answer seemed to be to make peace.

Mangas said he would talk with the White Eyes. Geronimo begged his chief not to go – he didn't trust them. But Mangas went. One evening he walked into the White Eyes' camp.

By the morning he was dead.

The White Eyes tortured him before they killed him. They set red-hot blades of steel against his bare feet. They said that Mangas had tried to escape so they shot him. And then they cut off his head, boiled it and sent his skull to a professor in Boston.

This was the worst horror of all. Apaches believed that a man would enter the spirit world in the same state in which he had left this one. With his head cut from his body, Mangas Coloradas would suffer forever.

And the White Eyes would be punished for it. Cochise and Geronimo would see to that.

Chapter 6
Fighting Back

When the American Civil War was over settlers came pouring into New Mexico and Arizona. Gold miners returned to Pinos Altos. The miners found silver close by and Silver City sprang up. The area was booming.

The US government thought that the land was theirs and they could use it as they wanted. They believed it was their God-given right to settle across all of North America – from "sea to shining sea".

The government wanted to put the Apache tribes on to reservations – special areas of land set aside for Indians to live on. That way the government could count and control them. Apaches had to stay where they were told. They were not allowed to leave the reservation, not even to hunt. The government ordered the tribes to change their way of life and become farmers.

But the Apaches resisted. They wanted to keep their freedom. They wouldn't give it up without a fight.

The mood of the settlers pouring into the territory was ugly. In 1871 a mob from Tucson attacked an unarmed Indian camp. They raped and murdered 144 people, who were mostly women and children.

The white men who'd done it were arrested and put on trial but the white jury didn't find a single one of them guilty.

****

When the army built a fort by the spring in Apache Pass, Cochise and his people kept to the mountains. Geronimo moved freely between the Apache tribes. For a time he was with Cochise in his mountain home. From there the men went on fighting, attacking and then scattering to escape from the soldiers who chased them. They would re-group to fight once more in the rough, wild country they knew so well.

But things were changing fast. Cochise was ill and the future looked more and more grim. Tom Jeffords was the only white man Cochise trusted. In 1872 he let Tom Jeffords bring a soldier called General Howard to his camp for peace talks.

Howard told Cochise that if they stopped fighting, his people could return to Apache Pass and live in peace on their own land.

Cochise answered, "You tell me we can stay in our mountains and our valleys. That is all we wish. We do not want to fight and kill whites, and we do not want the whites to fight and kill us. We want nothing but to live in peace. But I do not believe you will allow us to remain on the lands we love."

"I warn you, if you try to move us again war will start once more. It will be a war without end, a war in which every Apache will fight until he is dead. Prove to me that I am wrong. Prove to me that this time I can trust you."

Howard made a solemn promise to Cochise but Cochise had been right not to trust the white man. While he was alive, his tribe was safe but he died in 1874. And in

1876 the US government ordered Cochise's people to leave their homeland.

Chapter 7
San Carlos

It was a place no white settler wanted. A place no Indian could live. A barren desert where only rattle-snakes and scorpions could stand the blistering heat. There was no game to hunt, no nuts or fruits to harvest. The warm water of the sluggish river that flowed through it was a breeding ground for mosquitoes that carried deadly malaria.

This was San Carlos. This was where the US government said the Apaches must now live.

In 1876 when the order came to move Cochise's people from Apache Pass to San Carlos, they didn't want to go. Juh's tribe were also living in Apache Pass at that time and they, too, were told to leave.

Cochise had died. His son, Taza, was now chief. But Taza was not the strong leader his father had been. When Taza agreed to go to San Carlos many of the Apaches turned to Juh. Geronimo was one of them.

Juh said he could offer nothing but hardship and death. If they did not do what the White Eyes wanted they would be called "hostiles" and "renegades". The soldiers would treat them as if they were criminals. If they did not go to the reservation they would be hunted like animals by troops from both the United States and Mexico. Juh told his followers that they must choose between death from heat, starvation and disease in

San Carlos or a life on the run in Mexico.
The new life would be short, maybe, but free.

Two thirds of the Apaches chose freedom.
700 of them slipped away at night, following
Juh and Geronimo into the mountains of
northern Mexico.

Chapter 8

"It takes an Apache to catch an Apache"

It was General George Crook who came up with the idea of using Apache scouts to hunt down the "renegades". Many of the white settlers thought he was mad. Pay Apaches to do the soldiers' work? That was crazy! Indians were wild! No one could trust them! In a battle the Indian scouts would join forces with the Apaches, wouldn't they? They'd swap sides and kill their white bosses. No one but a mad man would even think of such a thing!

Crook wasn't mad, but he was different from most whites. He knew that Apaches rode better, shot better and were far fitter than his American soldiers. What's more, they understood the land and their tracking skills were astonishing. Crook didn't make the mistake of thinking that all Indians were the same. He saw where there were clashes and quarrels and he made use of them.

There had always been problems between different Apache tribes. Even so, it wasn't easy to get one group to hunt down another.

Crook gave a long speech to the Apaches he wanted to work for him. He said the white people were crowding in and soon it would be impossible for anyone to live by hunting. The Apaches already knew this was true and so they listened to his words. Crook said it was far better for them to plant crops, and raise horses, cows and sheep. That way, he promised, the Apaches would soon be richer than the Mexicans! It was a tempting thought.

Next came the tricky part. Crook said that if any Apaches would not come into the reservations, he would expect the good men to help him bring in the bad ones. It was the way white people did things. If there were bad men in a town all the good men helped to arrest and punish them.

Crook's speech worked. He got his scouts. When they signed up for the US Army, it meant that Geronimo's days as a free Apache were coming to an end.

Chapter 9
The Last Break Out

"Run, ride, fight, hide, then ride and fight again." This was the way of life for a free Apache. They could only just survive. They couldn't win. There were too many White Eyes for that.

Over the next ten years Geronimo tried to settle down to reservation life. But it was hard. He had always been free. He'd lived his life as he wanted. Now his every move was watched.

The land the Apaches had been given to farm wasn't big enough. They needed food and clothes from the government too. They couldn't do anything without permission. And there was the constant fear of being killed as Mangas Coloradas and so many others had been.

Each time Geronimo tried to live on the reservation, things went wrong. And each time, he fled back to the mountains.

When Geronimo made his last escape the Apaches were split among themselves about what they should do. Many thought they had no choice – they had to adapt to the new way of life that had been forced on them. But there were others who still wanted to fight to the very end.

In 1885 Geronimo broke out for the fourth and last time. By then the great chiefs Geronimo had known were dead. Mangas

Coloradas had been murdered. Cochise and Juh had died. Another had been killed in a Mexican ambush.

Only a quarter of the tribe went with Geronimo – 35 men, eight boys old enough to fire a gun and 101 women and children. The group split into small bands and headed for the border. They went in different directions so that it was more difficult for the soldiers to follow their tracks.

The army chased them and at one point scouts managed to ambush the band Geronimo was with. In the attack they killed one boy and took nearly all of the women and children prisoner. Those who escaped would never be happy without their families. Two months later Geronimo agreed to meet General Crook.

Geronimo and the general talked for a long time. At last Geronimo said, "Once I

moved about like the wind. Now I surrender to you and that is all."

They shook hands on it. Crook thought that now there'd be peace.

But the Apache wars weren't over yet.

That night the men got so drunk that they could hardly move the next morning. They travelled only a short distance before they made camp once more.

By then Geronimo and his men had begun to think that Crook's promises might count for nothing. They might be as empty and worthless as every other white man's.

Before the next sunrise, Geronimo had vanished – along with 21 men, 14 women and six children. A party of soldiers and scouts was sent after them.

Geronimo later talked about the bravery of his small group of Apaches. "We felt that every man's hand was against us," he said. "If we returned to the reservation we would be put in prison and killed, if we stayed in Mexico they would continue to send soldiers to fight us." Geronimo's band knew they could expect no mercy. They gave none in return.

Crook had failed to bring in Geronimo. The US government put a new general in his place – General Miles. General Miles asked the government for 2,000 more soldiers to fight the "hostiles".

By 1886 Geronimo's band were the last Indians in the USA fighting for their freedom. They were hunted by 5,000 soldiers – a quarter of the US army – and 3,000 soldiers from Mexico. There were Indian scouts, too, and many groups of white settlers who were after them. In the end there were almost

9,000 armed men chasing a group of 34 Apaches.

Apache chiefs led their men and were always first in the firing line. The white generals sent their men into battle ahead of them while they stayed safely at the back. How cowardly this must have looked to the Apache fighters!

General Miles sent his men to guard every water hole, every pass and every ranch in the area. Then he sent Captain Henry Lawton with "one hundred of the strongest and best soldiers that could be found" to catch Geronimo.

Lawton's soldiers covered more than 3,000 miles in four months. It was a nightmare for them. Every day they marched in intense heat. The rocks burned and blistered their feet and their rifle barrels scalded their hands if they touched them. The rough

country was full of cacti and rattle-snakes and they had no idea how or where to find water. When the rain came, it came in torrents and turned dry canyons into swollen, angry rivers that could sweep men and horses away.

The soldiers were worn out. And in all that time they caught up with Geronimo only once. Even then, every Apache got away unhurt.

In their five months on the run, only one woman was shot – by a Mexican. One man slipped away and surrendered and another was killed when he was trying to trade in Mexico. Three or four times they lost their animals and supplies in Mexican attacks. When that happened, Geronimo's group took food and horses from where they could find them. In one raid, they killed 14 Americans. They killed more Mexicans – some say as many as 600 died that summer.

Geronimo's Power was very important to the whole band. One night they had to cross a flat plain where there was nowhere for them to hide. His men later spoke of how Geronimo's chanting had held back the sunrise so that they could escape while it was still dark.

His nephew said that Geronimo had to get food for his men, and for their women and children. When they were hungry, he fed them. When his people were cold, Geronimo fetched blankets and clothes. When they had no horses, he took them. When they had no bullets, he found them. "He was a good man."

But then General Miles asked two new Indian scouts to help him. They were brothers and cousins to some of Geronimo's men. General Miles sent them into Mexico with a small party of soldiers.

It looked hopeless. The mountains were huge. Geronimo's group was so small that they could stay hidden in the rocks forever. But then the scouts got lucky. Geronimo had sent two women into the town of Fronteras to say that their group wished to surrender. The women had been allowed to trade there, and gone back to the Indian camp with three new ponies and food and drink.

Both the Indians and the Mexicans had been lying. Geronimo was never going to surrender. He had only talked about peace to get more supplies. And the Mexicans had traded only to trick the rest of the Indians into town so that they could kill them all.

The scouts tracked the women for three days from Fronteras into the mountains. Then they walked towards Geronimo's camp.

Geronimo's nephew was on guard. He saw the scouts coming and told his uncle.

The men watched and waited as the scouts came nearer.

"If they come closer they are to be shot," said Geronimo.

"They are our brothers," one man answered. "Let's find out why they come. They are brave men to risk this."

Geronimo argued with him, but it was no good. "We will not shoot," the man said. "The first man who lifts a rifle I will kill."

"I will help you." Fun, one of the bravest, best Apache fighters spoke up. Geronimo had no choice.

"Let them come," he said.

The scouts entered the camp and one of them told the weary band, "The troops are coming after you from all directions. Their aim is to kill every one of you if it takes 50

56

years." He went on, "Everything is against you ... If you are awake at night and a rock rolls down the mountains or a stick breaks you will be running ... You even eat your meals running. You have no friends anywhere in the world." Then he told them, "I get plenty to eat. I go wherever I want ... I go to bed whenever I want and get all my sleep. I have nobody to fear."

The band agreed to a meeting with the US soldiers the next day. They met, they talked, but the Apaches were still unsure. For a long time they didn't know what they should do. At last Geronimo's cousin spoke. His family were on the reservation. "I am going to surrender." He said he loved his wife and children. "I want to be with them." A second, then a third man said the same.

Geronimo was silent. He knew how much he depended on those three men. "You have been great fighters in battle," he said at last.

"If you are going to surrender, there is no use my going without you. I will give up with you."

Geronimo never stopped feeling he had made the wrong decision. He should have died fighting in his homeland where he belonged.

The soldiers took Geronimo and his group back to General Miles. Miles told them, "Lay down your arms and come with me to Fort Bowie and in five days you will see your families." He promised them, "Everything you have done up to this time will be wiped out and forgotten, and you will begin a new life ... You will have a separate reservation with your tribe, your horses and wagons and no one will harm you."

Once again in the sad history of America the promise of a white man was empty and worthless and counted for nothing.

Geronimo's "renegades" were taken to Florida along with the rest of the Chiricahua Apaches. 500 men, women and children were held as prisoners of war. Even the Apache scouts who'd worked for the US army and helped to catch Geronimo were taken prisoner.

When the Apaches were moved from their lands it was as if their hearts had been ripped from them. They had always lived under the enormous open skies of Arizona. But they were held as prisoners of war in an area of dense forest. If they wanted to see the sky, they had to climb the trees.

And it was damp and warm. All around them were swamps where deadly mosquitoes swarmed. The Apaches were used to breathing the clean, dry air of Arizona. Many of them died from malaria or TB.

Their children were taken away to boarding schools so they could learn the ways of the white man.

Eight years later, the Apaches were moved to Fort Sill in Oklahoma but they were still prisoners.

In total, they were prisoners of war for 27 years. Before the start of the Indian Wars there were about 2,000 Chiricahua Apaches living in New Mexico and Arizona. In 1913, when they were set free at last, only 261 were still alive.

Near the end of his life, Geronimo had a private meeting with the American president. Geronimo told him, "My hands are tied as if with rope ... I pray you to cut the ropes and make me free. Let me die in my own country, an old man who has been punished enough."

The President did nothing. Geronimo died in 1909 without ever seeing his home-land again.

His enemies called him a cold-hearted killer, a dangerous criminal, the "worst Indian of them all".

His friends called him a good man, a brave fighter, a great leader, a hero.

Cold hearted criminal?

Hero?

You decide.

How far would you go to defend your freedom?

Timeline

1492   Christopher Columbus sets out to find a new way to India and "discovers" America instead. He calls the native people who come to meet him "Indians".

1519-1521   Cortes conquers Mexico and destroys the Aztec empire.

1540   The Spanish bring the first horses to North America.

1607   English settlers build their first town at Jamestown, Virginia.

1775-1783   The American Revolution. 13 states fight for independence from British rule. They win and the USA is born.

1776	The American Declaration of Independence declares that "all men are created equal" but it totally ignores the rights of its native peoples – the Indians who lived in North America before any European settlers arrived.
1821	Mexico becomes independent from Spain.
1829	Geronimo is born.
1845	"Manifest Destiny" justifies the white man's right to settle across the entire North American continent.
1850	Geronimo's family is killed by Mexican soldiers.
1853	The Gadsden Purchase. America buys land in New Mexico, Arizona

and California from Mexico. Settlers start to move in to the area.

1861 Bascom accuses Cochise of attacking a settler's ranch and kidnapping a child.

1861-1863 Apaches fight the White Eyes under the leadership of Cochise and Mangas Coloradas.

1863 Mangas Coloradas is murdered.

1861-1865 The American Civil War. The northern and southern states fight. When the war is over slavery is abolished.

1874 Cochise dies.

1876 The US government orders the removal of the Chiricahua Apaches from their land.

1886	Geronimo surrenders for the last time. The Chiricahua Apaches are transported to Florida and held as prisoners of war for 27 years.
1909	Geronimo dies.
1913	The 261 Chiricahua Apaches still alive are set free. But they are not allowed to go back to Arizona. Two thirds of them join the Mescalero Apaches on their reservation in New Mexico. The others stay in Oklahoma as the Fort Sill Apache tribe.
1924	The Indian Citizenship Act is passed, finally giving citizenship to all Native Americans.

AUTHOR CHECK LIST

Tanya Landman

What gave you the idea for this book?

A few years ago I wrote a book called *Apache*. When it was published I went all over the UK giving talks. I soon found out that no one knew much about the history of America. Some people didn't even know how thousands of white European immigrants had crossed the Atlantic to America to settle there.

Geronimo in 1887

Or that anyone else lived there first. Many thought an Apache was a helicopter or a computer program. They didn't know anything about the native American people. That's why I decided to write about Geronimo.

Was Geronimo the only great Indian warrior?

There were so many, I'd need another book to list them all. Each Indian tribe had its own extraordinary heroes – the Sioux had Sitting Bull and Crazy Horse who defeated General Custer at the Battle of the Little Bighorn in 1876. The Apaches had Cochise, Juh and Victorio whose sister Lozen was a woman warrior.

If you could meet Geronimo, what would you ask him?

Geronimo became very famous. In 1905, when Theodore Roosevelt was elected as US President he asked Geronimo to ride in his parade. I'd ask Geronimo how he really felt about that.

ILLUSTRATOR CHECK LIST

Seb Camagajevac

If you could time-travel, which period of history would you visit?

I'd like to go back to the beginning of the 1900s.

Which period of history would you not like to visit?

World War Two.

Have you been to America?

Yes, I've been to L.A. Driving through the city was pretty cool. Just like in the movies.

If you could meet Geronimo, what would you ask him?

How he kept on fighting all those years, and how he was strong enough to keep going.

Geronimo (right) with his fellow warriors in 1886

Barrington Stoke would like to thank all its readers for commenting on the manuscript before publication and in particular:

Cynthia Clift
Charlie Court
Patrick Dixon
Lee Gunton
Alex Heath
Ben Jackson
Christopher Naiefel
Serena Naismith
Kabilas Parameswaran
Daniel Sibthorpe

Become a Consultant!

Would you like to be a consultant? Ask your parent, carer or teacher to contact us at the email address below – we'd love to hear from them! They can also find out more by visiting our website.

schools@barringtonstoke.co.uk
www.barringtonstoke.co.uk

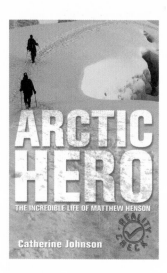

Arctic Hero
by
Catherine Johnson

At the North Pole Matthew Henson battled fear, frostbite and freezing winds. At home in America, he was treated badly – just because he was black. But Matt never gave up ... The amazing adventure of Matthew Henson. Explorer. Survivor. Arctic Hero.

The Day the Island Exploded
by Alexandra Pratt

It's the trip of a life-time! Graham's on an island – deep in frozen Antarctica. But one day the ground starts to rumble.
The volcanoes are erupting!
The island is exploding ...
Can he escape in time?

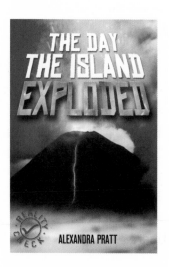

You can order these books directly from our website at
www.barringtonstoke.co.uk

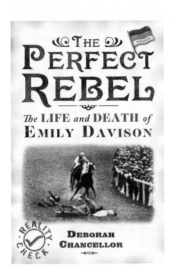

**The Perfect Rebel
by
Deborah Chancellor**

Emily Davison wanted votes for women. She threw stones, and set fires, and blew up a house. She went to prison many times. She risked her life for the vote, and in the end she died for it.
Was she a terrorist?
Was she a hero?
Time for a Reality Check.

**Snow Tigers
by
Simon Chapman**

Snow storms. Forest fires. Armed robbers. Deep in the forests of Siberia, the Captain has to face them all. But in the shadows lurks something much more deadly ... the snow tigers.

You can order these books directly from our website at
www.barringtonstoke.co.uk